A GARLAND OF GEMS OF WISDOM FOR A HAPPY AND SUCCESSFUL LIFE

[Maxims, Precepts, Proverbs, and Thoughts]

A GARLAND OF GEMS OF WISDOM FOR A HAPPY AND SUCCESSFUL LIFE

[Maxims, Precepts, Proverbs, and Thoughts]

K.C.N. Nair & Shantha N. Nair

Commonwealth

A Garland of Gems of Wisdom for
A Happy and Successful Life

First Published 2005

ISBN 81-311-0049-9

Published by:
Ajay Verma
For Commonwealth Publishers
4831/24, Prahlad Street,
Ansari Road, Darya Ganj,
New Delhi - 110 002
Ph.: 23272541, 23257835
Fax : 91-011-23257835
e-mail-campusbooks@hotmail.com

Typesetting by:
Stylish Laser Typesetter
Delhi - 110053

Printed at:
Roshan Offset Printers
Delhi

Preface

The habit of jotting down striking Maxims, Precepts, and Proverbs which we came across while reading articles, magazines, and books over the past several years made us think, now, in the twilight of our life span, to publish them in the form of a small book. In this endeavor our son and our daughter-in-law have also helped us a great deal. It is our earnest desire and hope that these Gems of wisdom contained in this book will benefit all those who read this collection with a genuine interest. What man desires in his life is nothing but happiness and success. This book, if read and followed properly with discretion, we are sure, will help every one in paving a way for a better today and tomorrow.

It is with a sense of guilt that we have to admit that a number of Maxims and Precepts found here do not contain the names of those great ones who gave them. Our due apologies to them for this lapse. However, we wish to make it very clear, that this omission, though not the least negligible is never deliberate or an oversight, but inevitable as either we did not note down the names of those who stated them or the names were not available to us. In certain other cases we had taken their ideas in the way we understood them. As these are the reasons, we are sure, our readers will excuse us for this lacuna. Nevertheless if the readers are able to help us with the information, we will be ever grateful to them. We are sure to acknowledge their help individually with gratitude, in our next venture.

In addition this book also contains a few stray thoughts of ours, which our life over the years has taught us and we thought of sharing these 'Silver Streaks', if we may call them so, with our readers by including them here in this book.

We owe our gratefulness to all those known and unknown wise men who gave their valuable and precious revelations, which were born out of their wisdom to us. If this book is able to bring about any difference for better at least for a few of the readers, and make their life more successful and happier, we feel our mission is more than fulfilled and our life has been purposeful and also we get the satisfaction that we are able to contribute something to humanity, though in a limited manner. Thank God.

K.C.N. Nair & Shantha N. Nair

Contents

A

A bird in hand is worth two in the bush.

A blow with a word strikes deeper than a blow with a sword.

—Robert Burton

A bore talks mostly in the first person, a gossip in the third and a brilliant conversationalist in the second.

—Anonymous

A broken hand works but not a broken heart.

—Persian Proverb

A cheerful friend is like a sunny day shedding brightness on all around.

—Sir John Lubock

A clear conscience fears no accusation.

A closed mouth catches no flies.

—Italian Proverb

A constant guest is never welcome.

A danger foreseen is half avoided.

—Thomas Fuller

A drowning man is not troubled by rain.

—Persian Proverb

A duty, which becomes a desire, will ultimately become a delight.

—George Gritter

A fault confessed is half redressed.

A fault once denied is twice committed.

A favourable wind will not blow forever. So be cautious.

A few heart—whole, sincere and energetic men can do more in a year than a mob in a century.

—Vivekananda

A flatterer is a dangerous person. Avoid him.

A flatterer is a secret enemy.

A flow of words is no proof of wisdom.

A fool may ask more questions in one hour than a wise man can answer in seven years.

A friend in need is a friend in deed.

—English Proverb

A friend is a second self.

—Aristotle

A friend is one who knows all about you and likes you just the same.

A friend's eye is a good mirror.

—Irish Proverb

A full cup must be carried steadily.

—English Proverb

A gem cannot be polished without frictions nor man perfected without trials.

—Lobsong Rampa

A genius is one who shoots at something no one else can see and hits it.

—George Herbert

A genius observes and does not talk unnecessarily .

A gift with a kind countenance is a double gift.

A good example is the best sermon.

A good face needs no paint.

A good friend never offends.

A good laugh is the world's best tonic.

A good leader inspires other men with confidence in him;

a great leader inspires them with confidence in themselves.

A good liar needs good memory.

—Arabic Proverb

A good life is life eternal.

A good name is sooner lost than won.

A good score is worth more to a man than good advice.

—Amiel

A good servant makes a good master.

A good tongue is a good weapon.

A great flame follows a little spark.

—Alighieri

A great man who is able to handle his mind is able to handle the world.

A great talker is a great liar.

A guilty conscience is a hidden enemy.

A guilty conscience needs no accuser.

A happy home is one in which each spouse grants the possibility that the other may be right, though neither believes it.

—Frazer

A happy life consists in tranquility of mind.

—Cicero

A hasty man is seldom out of trouble.

A healthy mind in a healthy body.

—Juvenal

A hero is one who knows how to hang on one minute longer.

A hero is someone who has given his or her life to something bigger than oneself.

—Joseph Campbell

A journey of a thousand miles must begin with a single step.

—Lao-tzu

A judicious Silence is always better than truth spoken with out clarity.

—De Sales

A just war is better than an unjust peace.

A kingdom founded on injustice never lasts.

—Seneca

A lie can travel half way around the world while the truth is putting on its shoes.

—Mark Twain

A lie has speed but truth has endurance.

A little leak will sink a great ship.

A little learning is a dangerous thing.

A little oil may save a great deal of friction.

A living dog is better than a dead lion.

A loan though old is not a gift.

—Hungarian Proverb

A lock is better than suspicion.

—Irish Proverb

A lost inch of gold may be found; a lost inch of time never.

—Chinese Proverb

A lot of time, effort, perseverance and sacrifice are required to climb up. But the fall does not require any of these and it is so sudden.

A man does not seek his luck, luck seeks its man.

—Turkish Proverb

A man in debt is caught in a net.

A man is a hero not because he is braver than anyone else but because he is brave for ten minutes longer.

—Emerson

A man is known by what he loves—friends, places, books, thoughts; good or bad. From these his character is told.

—Rev. Dr. Edgar Tilton

A man may die, nations may rise and fall, but an idea lives on. Ideas have endurance with out death.

—John. F. Kennedy

A man of words and not of deeds is like a garden full of weeds.

—Anonymous

A man should not be judged by the nature of his duties; but by the manner in which he does them.

A man who can keep his head and his temper and his friendliness when things are going wrong has poise.

A minute's success pays the failure of years.

—Robert Browning

A miser grows rich by seeming poor; an extravagant man grows poor by seeming rich.

A miser spends all his life adding, multiplying and subtracting—his grateful relatives divide.

A new groom sweeps clean but the old brush knows all the corners.

—Irish Proverb

A noble heart never forces itself forward. Its words are as rare gems, seldom displayed and of great value.

—Zengetsu

A patient listener attracts people.

A penny saved is a penny gained.

—Scottish Proverb

A pessimist is a liability to others.

A promise is a debt.

A prudent man does not make the goat his gardener.

—Hungarian Proverb

A prudent person profits from personal experience, a wise one from the experience of others.

A pupil who is a slave to his study becomes its master.

A really great man is known by three signs. . . generosity

in the design, humanity in the execution, moderation in success.

—Bismark

A really great man is simple and true.

—M. Currie

A rolling stone gathers no moss.

A rumour goes in one ear and out many mouths.

—Chinese Proverb

A silent mouth is melodious.

—Irish Proverb

A simple man lives low; a learned man things high; a spiritual seeker couples the simple living with high thinking.

A sincere friend is one who will say nasty things to your face instead of saying them behind your back.

A single fact is worth a shipload of argument.

A slippery mouth worketh ruin.

A simple acts upon difficulties as the sun upon the clouds. It disperses them.

—Mother

A smile does not cost anything, but pays big dividends. Not only does it make you feel good but it makes every one else feel better too.

A smile is a curve that can straighten many things.

A smile is an inexpensive way to improve your looks.

A smile is the lighting system of the face and the healing system of the heart.

A smile not only increases your face value but also improves the mood of the person at whom it is flashed.

A society grows great when old men plant trees whose shade they know they shall never sit in.

—Greek Proverb

A soft answer turneth away wrath; but grievous words stir up anger.

—Bible

A sound mind in a sound body

—Juvenal

A spoon does not know the taste of soup, nor a learned fool the taste of wisdom.

—Welsh Proverb

A stitch in time saves nine.

A successful man is one who can lay a firm foundation with the bricks that others throw at him.

—Chinmayananda

A successful life does not wait for opportunity to overtake it. It finds opportunities every day.

—Anon

A sunny temperament gives out an aroma, the fragrance of which fills the air with the odours of paradise.

A sunny temperament is a talisman more powerful than wealth; more precious than rubies.

A teacher affects eternity; he can never tell where his influence stops.

A teacher is better than two books.

—German Proverb

A thing of beauty is a joy forever.

—John Keats

A thorn defends the rose, harming only those who would steal the blossom.

—Chinese Proverb

A true critic is like a true friend because he plays the part of a mirror. He shows you as you are.

A true friend is the one who comes in when the whole world has gone out.

A truth that is told with bad intent beats all the lies you can invent.

—William Blake

A warm and intimate smile makes the hardest attitudes disappear and brings friendly and immediate response.

A weak foundation destroys the work.

A wise man can see more from the bottom of a well than a fool can from a mountain top.

A wise man goes slowly but arrives surely at his goal.

A wise man makes his own decisions; an ignorant man follows the public opinion.

—Chinese Proverb

A wise man gets more use from his enemies than a fool from his friends.

—Gracian

A wise man never looks for opportunities but creates them.

A word spoken is an arrow let fly.

A word to the wise is enough.

—Plautus

A work ill done must be done twice.

A wound from a tongue is worse than a wound from a sword, for the latter affects only the body, the former the spirit.

—Pythagoras

A young tree bends; an old tree breaks.

Ability has no school.

—Turkish Proverb

Absolute power corrupts absolutely.

Act well your part; there all the honour lies.

Action is life. Inaction is death. We must be doers not dreamers.

Actions speak louder than words.

Adversity does teach who your real friends are.

—Biyold

Adversity is the only balance to weigh friends.

After clouds comes clear weather.

Against criticism a man can neither protest nor defend himself; he must act inspite of, and then it will gradually yield to him.

—Von Goethe

Age is honourable and youth is noble.

—Irish Proverb

Age is no guarantee of maturity.

—Blackwell

All appears to change when we change.

—Amiel

All human actions have one or more of these seven causes : chance, nature, compulsion, habit, reason, passion and desire.

—Aristotle

All love is life. All selfishness is death.

—Vivekananda

All that glitters is not gold.

All that is worth cherishing in this world begins in the heart, not the head.

All things grow with time, except grief.

All truths are not to be told.

—English Proverb

All truths passes through three stages. First, it is ridiculed. Second, it is violently opposed. Third, it is accepted as being self-evident.

—Arthur Schopenhauer

Allow others to talk about themselves.

Always have self-confidence.

Always have when you can. It is cheap medicine.

—Lord Byron

Always remember to say 'Thank You'.

An active mind is the best insurance against boredom depression and morbid fears.

—Adler

An acute word cuts deeper than a sharp weapon.

—Thomas Fuller

An age builds up cities; an hour destroys them.

—Seneca

An angry man is not fit to pray.

An eye for an eye makes the whole world blind.

—Gandhiji

An honest man's word is as good as his bond.

An idle brain is a devil's workshop.

An injury is much sooner forgiven than an insult.

—Chester Field

An injury forgiven is better than an injury revenged.

An optimist laughs to forget, a pessimist forgets to laugh.

An optimist sees an opportunity in every calamity; a pessimist sees a calamity in every opportunity.

An ounce of vanity spoils a hundred pounds of merit.

Anger and intolerance are the twin enemies of correct understanding.

—Gandhiji

Anger dies quickly with a good man.

Anger harms you long before it harms the other person.

Anger is short madness.

Anger manages everything badly.

Anger so clouds the mind, that it cannot perceive the truth.

—Cato The Elder

Angery words fan the fire like wind.

Any man on any day is a fool for five minutes, but wisdom lies in not exceeding that five minutes.

—Mark Twain

Any man can be ignorant, but he must not be ignorant of his own ignorance.

— Mark Twain

Any one can hold the helm when the sea is calm.

—Syrus

Any one can make a mistake. A fool insists on repeating it.

Any word, every world in language, every circumstance, becomes poetic in the hands of a higher thought.

—Emerson

Arise, Awake and stop not till the goal is reached.

—Vivekananda

As a man thinketh in his heart, so is he.

As a well-spent day brings happy sleep, so life well used brings happy death.

—Leonardo Vinci

As long as you have anything, you owe something to those who have nothing.

—Vinoba Bhave

As the mind so the world.

As the water shapes itself to the vessel that contains it, so a wise man adapts himself to circumstances.

—Confucius

As you make your character so will you shape your life.

As you sow, you reap.

Associate with people of good quality if you esteem your reputation, for, it is better to be alone than to be in bad company.

—George Washington

Avoid negative influences and laziness.

B

Barking does seldom bite.

Be ambitious but not dissatisfied.

Be ambitious but not over ambitious.

Be an optimist always.

Be bold to say, "I do not know "about things which you really do not know.

Be broad-minded to admit your mistakes.

Be cautious but not over cautious.

Be civil to all; sociable to many, familiar with a few, friend to one, enemy to none.

—*Benjamine Franklin*

Be committed to the work you undertake.

Be concerned about the interests of children, needs of youth, and comforts of the old.

Be confident but not over confident.

Be courteous to all, but intimate with a few, and let those few be well tried before you give them your confidence.

—*George Washington*

Be economical but not miserly.

Be extravagant in giving love.

Be frank but not rude.

Be friendly towards others and friends will soon flock around you.

Be firm but not rude.

Be generous in honest and sincere appreciation.

Be gentle and modest, but do not hesitate to be firm when the situation demands.

Be gentle but not meek.

Be grateful to God for all the blessings.

Be humble and confident but not proud and over confident.

Be humble, give up your pride, sit at the feet of the wise and learn a bit.

Be liberal but not extravagant.

Be liberal in appreciating every thing that is good.

Be not afraid of going slowly; be afraid only of standing still.

Be quick but not hasty.

Be silent as to services you have rendered, but speak of favours you have received.

—Seneca

Be slow in choosing, but slower in changing.

Be slow to promise but quick to perform.

Be sober and temperate, and you will be healthy.

—Franklin

Be softer than the flower where kindness is concerned; be stronger than the thunder where principles are at stake.

Bear defeat courageously without losing heart and rise again.

Bear injustice without a slight retaliation.

Bear troubles, dangers, and grief with patience.

Beauty is power; a smile is its sword.

—Charles Reade

Begin removing small stones to remove big mountains.

Behaviour is a mirror in which everyone shows his image.

Being ignorant is not so much a shame as being unwilling to learn to do things the right way.

—Benjamin Franklin

Believe not that which any man said, not even I, the Lord Buddha, unless it appears to your common sense. And even then do not believe it, but treat it as a reasonable hypothesis, until such time as you can prove it for yourself.

—Buddha

Believe you are defeated; believe it long enough and it is likely to become a fact.

—Peale

Better an ugly face than an ugly mind.

—James Ellis

Better be alone than be in bad company.

Better be wise by the misfortunes of others than by your own.

—Aesop

Better bend than break.

—Scottish Proverb

Better do it than wish it done.

Better give a penny, than lend twenty.

—Italian Proverb

Better late than never.

"Better late than never" is not half so good a maxim as "Better never late".

—Pericles

Better to get up late and be wide-awake than to get up early and be asleep all day.

—Anonymous

Better to keep a friend than win an argument.

Better to light a candle than to curse the darkness.

—Chinese Proverb

Beware lest you lose the substance by grasping at the shadow.

—*Aesop*

Beware of little expenses; a small leak sinks a great ship.

—*Benjamin Franklin*

Beware of a silent dog and still water.

—*German Proverb*

Bitter pills will have blessed effects.

Blessed is he who expects nothing, for he shall never be disappointed.

—*Alexander Pope*

Blessings are not valued till they are gone.

Blood is thicker than water.

—*English Proverb*

Borrowed garments never fit well.

Borrowed money can never bring sound security.

Both attachment and detachment perfectly developed make a man great and happy.

—*Vivekananda*

Brevity is a great charm of eloquence.

Brining unity among diversity is wisdom.

Burn not your house to fright away the mice.

Butterflies often forget that they were once caterpillars.

By lowering your voice, your raise yourself.

By other's faults wise men correct their own.

By the work one knows the workmen.

—*Jean Fontaine*

C

Call on God but row away from the rocks.

Calmness of mind does not mean you should stop your activity. Real calmness should be found in activity itself.

Caution is the eldest child of wisdom.

—*Victor Hugo*

Caution is the parent of safety.

Character is man's greatest need and man's greatest safeguard.

—*Spencer*

Character may be manifested in great moments, but it is made in the small ones.

—*Brookes*

Charity begins at home.

Charity sees the need not the cause.

—*German Proverb*

Charm is more than beauty.

—*Yiddish Proverb*

Charm Strikes the sight, but goodness wins the soul.

Cheerfulness and contentment are great beautifiers and are famous preserves of youthful looks.

Cheerfulness is health.

Cheerfulness when kept as a principle against all odds is the finest form of courage.

Child is the father of man.

Circumstances are the rulers of the weak, but the instruments of the wise.

Circumstances have rarely favoured famous men. They have fought their way to triumphs through all sorts of opposing obstacles.

—*Milton*

Cleanliness is next to godliness.

Clouds gather before a storm.

Commitment to quality will be rewarded.

Communicate cheerfulness.

Concentrate on what we have got rather than on what we do not have.

Concentration and dedication are a must for success.

Conduct has the loudest tongue.

Confidence is the feeling that God is in me and egoism is the feeling that I am God.

Confidence is the touchstone of success.

—*Vivekananda*

Conscience is God's presence in man.

Consider failures not as hurdles but as stepping-stones to success.

Consorting with the wise will make you wise.

—*Menander*

Contentment is another name for the harmony of the mind.

Continuous industry, high ambition, great enthusiasm and excellent commonsense will be rewarded with success.

Control anger. It harms you even before it harms the other person.

Control over emotions is a mark of a great person.

Convert ideas in to action through seat and effort to accomplish the goal.

Count your blessings not hardships.

Courage consists not in blindly overlooking danger but in seeing and conquering it.

—Richter

Courage is contagious. When a brave man takes a stand the spines of others are stiffened.

—Graham

Courage is resistance to fear, mastery of fear—not absence of fear.

—Mark Twain

Courtesy costs nothing but buys everything.

Courtesy costs nothing, yet it pays bigger dividends to those who posses it than any other requisite.

—Chalmers

Courtesy is the best inheritance.

Courtesy is the hallmark of a successful man.

Courtesy is the sister of charity, which quenched hate and kept love alive.

Cowards die many times before their death; the valiant never taste of death but once.

—Shakespeare

Create happiness for others.

Creation is only the projection in to form of that which already exists.

Cultivate winning attitude.

Cut your coat according to your cloth.

Cultivate your temper to suit any circumstance in life.

D

Dare to do right, fear to do wrong.

Deal with the faults of others as gently as with your own.

—*Chinese Proverb*

Debt is the worst poverty.

Deeper the roots stronger the tree.

Defer not charities till death.

Desire and wants in themselves are not harmful. Adopt fair means to fulfill them so that the means you adopt are not unfair and harmful to others.

Diamond cuts diamond.

Difficulties don't crush a man—they make him.

Difficulties strengthen the mind as labour does the body.

—*Seneca*

Dig a well before you are thirsty.

—*Chinese Proverb*

Dignity consists not in possessing honours but in the consciousness that we deserve them.

—*Aristotle*

Diligence is the mother of good fortune.

Diligence is the mother of wisdom.

Diplomacy is thinking twice before saying nothing.

Diplomats and crabs are creatures who move in such a way that it is impossible to tell whether they are coming or going.

Discretion in speech is more than eloquence.

—*Bacon*

Discretion is the better part of valour.

Distant hills are evergreen.

Distance lends enchantment to the view.

Dive deep in to the ocean to get the pearls of wisdom.

Divide and rule a sound motto; Unite and lead a better one.

—*Gothe*

Do a good deed in secret and have it discovered by an accident.

Do all the good you can, by all the means you can, in all the ways you can, in all the places you can, at all the times you can, to all the people you can as long as ever you can.

—*Anonymous*

Do good to thy friend to keep him; to thy enemy to gain him.

—*Benjamin Franklin*

Do not allow a desire to become a craving. Inability to fulfill a desire may only disappoint you. But not getting a thing you crave for may shatter you completely.

Do not allows a little dispute to spoil great friendship.

Do not allow a trivial misunderstanding to wither the blossoms of spring.

—*Dickens*

Do not allow age to be a deterrent to accomplishments.

Do not anticipate trouble or worry about what may never happen.

—*Franklin*

Do not be afraid of going slowly; but be afraid of standing still.

Do not count you chickens before they are hatched.

—*Aesop*

Do not cut down the tree that gives you shade.

—Arabian Proverb

Do not fall before you are pushed.

—English Proverb

Do not feel ashamed to apologise for your faults. You must be ashamed of yourself only if you try to cover your faults.

Do not forget to say 'please' and 'thank you.'

Do not ignore little expenses. Even a small leak can sink a great ship.

Do not let negative people influence you.

Do not look up to others to make decisions for you. It will only weaken you.

Do not look where you fell but where you slipped.

—African Proverb

Do not make important decisions when you are physically or mentally upset.

Do not postpone charities till death.

Do not protect yourself by a fence, but rather by your friends.

—Czech Proverb

Do not put off important things to fiddle with trivialities.

Do not start a business unless you like to smile.

Do not try to impress others. Let them have the fun of impressing you.

Do not wait for inspiration. Even for a genious it is 99% perspiration and 1% inspiration.

Do not wait for opportunities, but create them for achieving excellence.

Do the best and leave the rest.

—Chinmayananda

Do unto others as you would have them do un to you.

Do your duty even when you are not being watched.

Doing good to others is not a duty. It is a joy, for it increases your own health and happiness.

—*Zoroastar*

Don't be penny wise and pound-foolish.

Don't hesitate to defend your dignity when the situation arises.

Don't let a little dispute injure a great friendship.

Don't lose self-confidence.

Drop by drop fills the tub.

—*French Proverb*

Drown not thyself to save a drowning man.

—*Thomas Fuller*

During conversation address a person by his or her name and use it as often as you can.

E

Each of us must become a spring at which men can quench their consuming thirst for appreciation.

—*Schweitzer*

Each word of kindness come whence it may is welcome to the poor.

—*Long Fellow*

Economise now so that you will not agonise later.

Economy is the wealth of the poor and the wisdom of the rich.

Educating the mind without educating the heart is no education at all.

—*Aristotle*

Education is not merely the road to earning a living but the gateway to knowledge, which makes living worthwhile.

Education is a wealth, which cannot be stolen away from its possessor.

Efficiency is the capacity to bring proficiency into expression.

—*Chinmayananda*

Effort is the expression of will power and is a master key to self-discipline.

Empty vessels make a lot of noise.

Endure trials patiently.

Enemies are the first to discover your mistakes.

Enjoy the present day trusting very little to the morrow,

—Horace

Enjoy when you can, and endure when you must.

—Von Goethe

Enquire not what boils an another's pot.

—Thomas Fuller

Envy shoots at others, but hits itself.

Even a revolution is an evolution.

Every action generates a force of energy that returns to us in like kind. . .what we sow is what we reap, and when we choose actions that bring happiness and success to others, the fruit of our karma is happiness and success.

—Vivekananda

Every artist dips his brush in his own soul, and paints his own nature in to his pictures.

—Beecher

Every body lights up a room. Some when they enter and some when they leave.

Every charitable act is a stepping-stone to heaven.

—Beecher

Every dark cloud has a silver lining.

Every day is a new birth in time holding out new beginnings, new possibilities, and new achievements.

—James Allen

Every difficulty is a test of courage; every failure a trial of strength.

Every dog has its day.

Every duty is holy, and devotion to duty is the highest form of the worship of God.

—Vivekananda

Every failure is a step to success.

Every garden may have some weeds.

—English Proverb

Every generation laughs at the old fashions, but follows religiously the new.

—*David Thoreau*

Every language is a temple in which the soul of those who speak it is enshrined.

—*Holmes*

Every man is the architect of his own fortunes.

—*Sallust*

Every moment dies a man.

Every moment one is born.

—*Tennyson*

Every one has a will to win but very few have the will to prepare to win.

—*Lombardi*

Every one loves the tree that gives him shelter.

—*Russian Proverb*

Every one should be the censor of his own consciousness.

—*Spellman*

Every one thinks of changing the world but no one thinks of changing himself.

—*Leo Tolstoy*

Every soul is a sun covered over with clouds of ignorance.

—*Vivekananda*

Every thing has its beauty but not every one sees it.

—*Confucius*

Everything is funny as long as it happens to someone else.

Every word man's lips have uttered echoes in God's skies.

—*Procter*

Evil to him who evil thinks.

Examine all things and hold fast that which is good.

—*St. Paul*

Examine what is said and not who speaks.

—*Arabic Proverb*

Excellence is not an aptitude but a habit.

Excuses are the nails used to build a house of failures.

—Mother Teresa

Experience is the father of wisdom.

—Anonymous

Experience is yesterday's answers to today's problems.

Experience is not what happens to a man. It is what a man does with what happens to him.

—Huxley

Experience is the best teacher.

Experience is the mother of wisdom.

F

Face is the index of the mind.

Face misfortunes with courage and try to turn it in to your advantage.

Facts do not cease to exist because they are ignorant.

—*Anonymous*

Facts speak for themselves.

Failures and disappointments in life should serve as inspiration.

Failure is a detour, not a dead end street.

Failure is the stepping-stone to success.

Faith puts us in touch with infinite power, opens the way to unbounded possibilities, limitless achievements.

—*Swettmardon*

Faith can achieve miracles while vanity or egoism is the death of man.

—*Ramakrishna Paramahamsa*

Faith is the bird that sings when the dawn is still dark.

—*Tagore*

Faith is to believe, what you do not see, the reward of which is you see, what you believed.

—*Chinmayananda*

False friends are worse than open enemies.

Familiarity breeds contempt.

—*Aesop*

Far too many things in life are snatched by the insincere. But we need not be dejected for sincerity always brings rewards peculiarly and richly its own.

—*Anon*

Fear always springs from ignorance.

—*Emerson*

Fear less, hope more.

Fear of obstacles is a hurdle to success.

Feel happy about the success of other, as you are about your own.

Few words to the wise suffice.

Fire and water are good servants, but bad masters.

Fire is the test of gold, adversity, of strong men.

—*Seneca*

First comes owing, and then comes lying.

Fist doubt, then inquire, then discover. This has been the process with all great thinkers.

—*H.T. Buckle*

Five things constitute virtue; they are courtesy, magnanimity, sincerity, earnestness and kindness. With courtesy, you avoid insult. With magnanimity, you win all. With sincerity, men will come to trust you. With earnestness and kindness, you can achieve success.

—*Confucius*

Flattery is like cologne water, to be smelt of, not swallowed.

—*Billings*

Flattery makes friends and truth makes enemies.

—*Spanish Proverb*

Follow great personalities; but do not imitate them.

For certain is death for the born.

And certain is birth for the dead.

Therefore over the inevitable.

Thou should not grieve.

—*Bhagavad Gita*

For him who has no concentration, there is no tranquility.

—*Bhagavad Gita*

For one man who sincerely pities our misfortune, there are a thousand who sincerely hate our success.

Force is all conquering, but its victories are short lived.

—*Abraham Lincoln*

Forget every act of kindness, and charity you do as soon as you have done it.

Forget injuries, never forget kindness.

—*Confucius*

Forget the benefit conferred; but remember the one you received.

Forget the slander you hear, before you can repeat it.

Forgive and forget the harm done by others.

Forgive the slight, the spit, and the sneer you face in your life.

Forsake not an old friend, for the new is not comparable to him. A new friend is as new wine, when is old thou shalt drink it with pleasure.

—*Old Testament*

Fortune favours the brave.

—*Virgil*

Four things come not back; the spoken word; the sped arrow; time passed; the neglected opportunity.

—*Halif*

Freedom implies restraint.

Freedom is not produced by a full enjoyment of what is desired, but controlling the desire.

—*Epictetus*

Friend in need is a friend in deed.

Friends are like melons

Shall I tell you why?
To find one good, you must
A hundred try.

—Mermet

Friends for the table are easy to find; but rare are those when danger is near.

—Laos Proverb

Friendship stops when borrowing begins.

—Sivananda

From lightest words sometimes the direst quarrel springs.

—Cato The Elder

From the end spring new beginnings.

G

Generosity is giving more than you can, and pride is taking less than you need.

Genius is creative.

Genius is infinite painstaking.

—Longfellow

Get rid of adverse thinking to remove mental blocks.

Getting along with others is the essence of getting ahead.

Give a man a fish and you feed him for a day. Teach a man to fish and you feed him for a lifetime.

—Chinese Proverb

Give as much as you can. Money, things, love, affection, respect and everything. But do not expect others to reciprocate or even recognize your actions. There lies your divinity.

Give credit where it is due.

Give every man thy ear, but few thy voice. Take each man's censure, but reserve the judgement.

—Shakespeare

Give the world the best you have and the best will come back to you.

Give yourself entirely to the divine to see the end of all your troubles.

Giving is superior to receiving.

Giving with cheerfulness is way to happiness.

God cannot go everywhere. So he made mothers.

God first, God last, God always.

God gives the nuts, but he does not crack them.

—German Proverb

God gives every bird its food, but He does not throw it in to the nest.

—J.G. Holland

God helps those who help themselves.

God is in every one. So if you try to love others, help others, make others happy, you are then loving God.

God is our refuge and strength, a very present help in trouble.

—Old Testament

God is within yourself. Dive within and realize.

God's delays are not God's denials.

Gold is tried by fire; brave men by adversity.

Good example is half the sermon.

—Anonymous

Good habits result from resisting temptations.

Good human relationships are essential for success.

Good is not good, where better is expected.

—Thomas Fuller

Good manners cost nothing but buys every thing.

Good manners without sincerity are like a beautiful dead lady.

—Yukteshwar

Good men carry their hearts on their tongues. Prudent men carry their tongues in their hearts.

—Turkish Proverb

Good parents give their children roots and wings. Roots to know where home is, wings to fly away and exercise what's being taught to them.

Good temper oils the wheels of life.

Good thoughts lead to good habits.

Good thoughts bear good fruit, bad thoughts bear bad fruit and man is his own gardener.

—James Allen

Good words are like a string of pearls.

—Chinese Proverb

Good words cool more than cold water.

—John Ray

Good words cost nothing but they are worth a lot.

Goodness becomes a lame virtue, if along with it there is no courage to endure everything.

—Mahatma Gandhi

Gossip cheapens the one who gossips more than the one gossiped about.

Gratitude is a fruit of great cultivation. You do not find it among gross people.

—Samuel Johnson

Gratitude not only the greatest of virtues, but the parent of all others.

—Cicero

Gratitude is the music of heart.

Gratitude is the sign of noble souls.

Great men are always good and simple.

Great minds discuss ideas, average minds discuss events and small minds discuss people.

—Rickover

Great occasions rouse even the lowest of human beings to some kind of greatness, but he alone is the really great man, whose character is always great, the same wherever he be.

—Vivekananda

Great people are not affected by each puff of wind that blows. Like great ships they sail serenely on, in a calm sea or a great tempest.

—George Washington

Great things are never achieved without enthusiasm.

Great things are not achieved easily.

Great things can be done by great sacrifices only.

—Vivekananda

Great thoughts reduced to practice, become great acts.

—Anon

Great thoughts live forever.

Great tranquility of heart is his who cares for neither praise nor blame.

—Kempis

Great works are performed, not by strength but by perseverance.

—Samuel Johnson

Greatness is never authoritative; it becomes the authority to which the later ages adore.

Greatness is not in being strong, but in the right use of strength.

—Beecher

Greed increases need.

H

Habit if not resisted soon becomes necessity.

Happiness comes to him who gives happiness to others.

—*Vivekananda*

Happiness comes when we work for the welfare of others.

Happiness depends on what you can give, not on what you can get.

—*Chinmayananda*

Happiness depends upon ourselves.

—*Aristotle*

Happiness gives us the energy, which is the basis of health.

—*Amiel*

Happiness is a perfume. You cannot shower it on others unless you have a drop of it on yourself.

Happiness is a wonderful commodity; the more you give, the more you have.

Hard words are harder than stones.

Hard work does not kill; It is worry that kills a person.

Harder the conflict, more glorious is the triumph.

Harshness breeds harshness like weeks in a barren field.

—*Buddha*

Haste makes waste.

Hate destroys a man's sense of values and his objectivity.

—*Martin Luther King Jr*

Hate less, love more.

Hate the sin not the sinner.

Hatred ever kills, love never dies.

Have a sunny temperament.

Have clear-cut priorities in life.

Have dignity of labour. Take pride in what you do.

Have compassion for the weak.

Have long range goals so that you will not be frustrated by short term failures.

Have the motivation to succeed in life.

Have the will to achieve your goal.

He approaches nearest to Gods who knows how to be silent, even though he is in the right.

— Cato The Elder

He doubles his gift who gives in time.

He doubly benefits the needy who gives quickly.

—Syrus

He gives double who gives unasked

—Arab Proverb

He gives twice who gives quickly.

He harms himself who does harm to another.

—Hesiod

He has enough who is content.

He is free from danger, who even when he is safe, is on his guard.

—Syrus

He is happy whose circumstances suit his temprer, but he is more excellent who can suit his temper to any circumstances.

—David Hume

He is not laughed at who laughs at himself first.

—Anonymous

He is strong who conquers others; He who conquers himself is mighty.

He knows much who knows how to hold his tongue.

He knows nothing who thinks he knows everything.

—Bernard Shaw

He of whom many are afraid ought to fear many.

—Bacon

He only employs his passion who can make no use of his reason.

—Cicero

He that always complains is never pitied.

He that blows in the dust, fills his eyes with it.

He that buys what he does not need must often sell what he does need.

He that can't endure the bad will not live to see the good.

—Jewish Proverb

He that climbs the tall tree has won the right to the fruit.

—Walter Scott

He that gives should never remember.

He that giveth should never remember; He that receives should never forget.

He that goes a borrowing goes a sorrowing.

He that is master of himself will soon be master of others.

He that is humble ever shall have God to be his guide.

He that is slow to anger is better than the mighty; and he that ruleth his spirit than he that taketh a city.

He that plants thorns must never expect to gather roses.

—English Proverb

He that receives should never forget.

He that runs fast will not run long.

He that says what he likes will hear what he doesn't like.

—Scottish Proverb

He that stays in the valleys will never get over the hill.

He who aims at the moon may hit at the top of the tree; He who aims at the top of a tree is unlikely to get off the ground.

He who begins many things finishes nothings.

—*Simmons*

He who cannot forgive others destroys the bridge over which he himself must pass.

He who does not become angry even in the worst circumstances, with God, human beings and beasts, has perfect forbearance.

—*Mahavira*

He who does not know how to dance says the floor is uneven.

He who fears being conquered is sure of defeat

—*Napolean*

He who feeds one hungry man is worthier than he who discourses on God and Heaven and truth and sin for a hundred years.

—*Buddha*

He who gives but does not smile, holds back half the gift.

He who has a perfect sense of true justice can claim the right to be obeyed.

—*Mother*

He who has health has hope and who has hope has everything.

—*Arabian Proverb*

He who has never hoped can never despair.

—*Bernard Shaw*

He who has no faith in himself can never have faith in God.

—*Vivekananda*

He who hesitates is lost.

He who is never satisfied can give no satisfaction to others.

He who is of calm and happy nature will hardly feel the pressure of age, but to him who is of an opposite disposition, youth and age are equally a burden.

—Plato

He who is slow to anger is better than the mighty and he who rules his spirit than he who takes a city.

He who is unable to rule over self can never really succeed in ruling over others.

He who knows does not speak.

He who knows how to obey knows how to command.

—Vivekananda

He who knows others is wise;

He who knows himself is enlightened.

—Lao-tzu

He who leaps high must take a long run.

—Danish Proverb

He who masters his passions conquers his greatest enemy.

He who never made a mistake never made a discovery.

We who reigns within himself and rules his passions, desires and fears is more than a king.

—John Milton

He who spares the wicked injuries the good.

—Seneca

He who speaks without modesty will find it difficult to make his words good.

—Confucius

He who swells in prosperity will shrink in adversity.

He who thinks himself the happiest man is really so. But he who thinks himself the wisest man is generally the greatest fool.

He, who wants to do a great deal of good at once, will never do anything.

—Samuel Johnson

He who wants to do good knocks at the gate; He who loves finds the gate open.

He who will not economise will have to agonise.

—Confucius

He who would climb the ladder must begin at the bottom.

—English Proverb

He who would live in peace must hear and see and say the least.

He who would search for pearls must dive below.

—Dryden

He who would travel happily must travel light.

Heath is not valued till sickness comes.

—Thomas Fuller

Hear twice before you speak once.

Hearts like doors will open with ease to very little keys.
And do not forget that two of these.
Are 'I thank you' and 'if you please'.

Heaven helps not the men who will not act.

Help thyself and God will help thee.

—Herbert

Higher the ambition, greater should be the perseverance and industry to achieve the goal.

Hills are green far away.

Honesty is no pride.

Honesty is the best policy.

—English Proverb

Hope and courage are the two bright diamonds in the crown of success.

Hope for the best, get ready for the worst, and then take what God chooses to send.

How a person masters his fate is more important than what his fate is.

—Vonttumboldt

Humility gains power by suffering.

Humility is not towards all. Severity is needed in dealing with the wicked.

Humility is not weakness.

Humility is the solid foundation of all virtues.

—Confucius

Hurry is only good for catching flies.

—Russian Proverb

Hygiene is two thirds of health.

—Lebanese Proverb

Ideas are the raw material to success.

If a man be great, even his dog will wear a proud look.

—Japanese Proverb

If a man does only what is required of him, he is a slave. If a man does more than is required of him he is a free man.

—Chinese Proverb

If a man wants to accomplish anything in this world, he must not be afraid of assuming responsibilities.

If for tranquil mind you seek, these things observe with care, of whom you speak, to whom you speak, and how, and when and where.

—Anonymous

If I can stop one heart from breaking I shall not live in vain.

—Emily Dickinson

If one speaks or acts with a cruel mind, misery follows, as the cart follows the horse, if one speaks or acts with a pure mind, happiness follows, as a shadow follows its course.

—Dharmapada

If people do not know much, do not laugh at them, for; every one of them knows somethings that you do not.

—Gypsy Proverb

If there is faith in the future, there is power in the present.

If there is light in the soul there will be beauty in the person.

If there is beauty in the person there will be harmony in the house.

If there is harmony in the house there will be order in the nation.

If there is order in the nation there will be peace in the world.

—Chinese Proverb

If thy aim be great, and thy means small, still act; for, by action alone these can increase to thee.

—Sri Aurobindo

If time is not favourable to thee, render thyself favourable to it.

—Turkish Proverb

If two men ride a horse, one must ride behind.

If we could see God in stone images, we should be able to see Him in living beings.

If we take care of the cause, the effect will take care of itself.

—Vivekananda

If wealthy be humble; plants bend when they have fruits.

—Saibaba

If winter comes, can spring be far behind?

If you are given to making fun of some one, be sure, it is yourself.

If you are not having problems, you are missing an opportunity for growth.

If you ask from within for peace, it will come.

If you can't do what you want, do what you can.

If you confer a benefit never remember it; if you receive it never forget it.

—Chilon

If you criticize others continuously for a certain fault of theirs, similar such tendencies which are dormant in your subconscious mind will be released and become active.

If you do not get what you like, like what you get.

If you do not like problems and challenges, you are missing an opportunity for growth.

If you do not sow in the spring you will not reap in the autumn.

—Irish Proverb

If you do not scale the mountain, you can not view the plain.

—Lobsang Rampa

If you feel down just consider that Sun sinks every night, but it rises every morning.

If you find a dream in your heart don't ever let it go; for, dreams can be tiny seeds from which tomorrow grow.

If you have not got any charity in your heart, you have the worst kind of heart trouble.

—Bob Hope

If you laugh at my face you laugh at God.

If you make a habit of seeing good in others, your inherent, dormant good tendencies will be released and come to the surface and they will be strengthen.

If you really put a small value upon yourself, rest assured that the world will not raise your price.

—Anonymous

If you refuse to be made straight when you are green, you will not be made straight when you are dry.

—African Proverb

If you scatter thorns, do not go bare foot.

—Italian Proverb

If you sit still, it is not your profits that will come to you but your expenses.

If you think you can or if you think you can't you are right.

—Henry Ford

If you want to be successful never lose hope.

If you wish success in life, make perseverance your bosom friend, experience your wise counselors, caution your elder brother and hope your guardian genius.

—Joseph Addison

It you wish to achieve a position in life, there is only one word that counts and that is work.

—T. Brown

If you wish to know the mind of a man, listen to his words.

—Chinese Proverb

If you wish to make a man your enemy, tell him simply "Your are wrong".

If you wish your merit to be known, acknowledge that of the other people

—Nigerian Proverb

If you worry about what people think of you, it indicates you have more confidence in their opinion than in your own.

If you would have good servants see that you be good masters

—Richard Baxter

If your desires be endless, you cares and fears will be so too.

—Thomas Fuller

If your dominant mental attitude is peaceable and lovable, bliss and blessedness will follow you.

—James Allen

If your foot slips you may recover your balance, but if your tongue slips, you cannot recall your words.

If your means suit not with your ends, pursue those ends which suit with your means.

Ignore the mistakes of others; if pointing out of the mistakes is essential, do it politely without wounding their feelings.

Ignore unjust criticisms.

Imagination is more important than knowledge.

—Albert Einstein

Imagination is the highest kite one can fly.

Impatience is a sign of immaturity.

In a river of tears count your blessings.

—Kubler Ross

In anger we should refrain both from speech and action.

—Pythagoras

In character, in manners, in all things the excellence is simplicity.

—Long Fellow

In charity there is no excess.

—Francis Bacon

In critical moments even the very powerful have need of the Weakest.

—Aesop

In every mistake there is a lesson.

In love, one and one are one.

In shallow men the fish of little thoughts cause much commotion; In oceanic minds the whales of inspiration make hardly a ruffle.

Instead of being jealous be happy about the success of others.

In taking revenge a man is but even with his enemy; but in passing it over he is superior; for it is a prince's part to pardon.

—Bacon

In the constant race of life there is no time to sit on the way side to mourn for the stones that we had crushed under our feet or the sharp thorn that had pierced ourselves. Eyes fixed to the goal, rush onward with positive determination and firm resolve.

—Chinmayananda

In the heart of a truly non-violent person there is a

profound belief that hate can only be driven out by love, that anger can only be conquered by compassion, and that fear can only be overcome by courage.

—Rajiv Gandhi

In the hour of adversity be not without hope, for crystal rainfalls from black clouds.

—Nizami

Industry keeps the body healthy, the mind clear, the heart whole and the purse full.

—Charles Simmons

Information is the seed for an idea and only grows when it is watered.

—Bergen

Injure others and you injure yourself.

—Lobsang Rampa

Innocence dwells with wisdom, but never with ignorance.

—William Blake

Instead of brooding over probiems, find solutions to it.

Instead of brooding over your wrong doings repent for it and make amends.

Instead of having the feeling of 'I, 'mine' and 'you' have the feeling of 'we', 'us' and 'ours', the result will be peace and happiness for one and all.

Intelligence and humility should go hand in hand.

Invention is the mother of necessity.

—Veblen

It does not matter how slowly you go so long as you do not stop.

—Confucius

It is a fact that the present depends on the past and the future is because of the present.

It is a fundamental rule of human life that if the approach is good, the response is also good.

It is a great mistake to fancy oneself greater than one is,

and to value oneself at less than one is worth.

—*Goethe*

It is a great thing to know our vices.

—*Cicero*

It is a great thing to know the season for speech and the season for silence.

—*Seneca*

It is a poor heart that never rejoices.

It is an all—too human frailty to suppose that a favourable wind will blow forever.

—*Rick Bode*

It is an inspiration to see people who are always cheerful.

It is better to be an army of sheep led by a tiger than an army of tigers led by a sheep.

It is better to change our opinion than to persist in a wrong one.

—*Socrates*

It is better to conceal one's knowledge than to reveal one's ignorance.

—*Spanish Proverb*

It is better to die on your feet than live on your knees.

It is better to do well than to say well.

It is books that teach us to refine our pleasures when young and to recall them with satisfaction when we are old.

It is concentration that builds careers, opens new worlds, brings forth innovations and carries on the business of the world.

It is foolish to fear what you cannot avoid.

—*Syrus*

It is foolish to tear one's hair in grief, as though sorrow would be made less with baldness.

—*Marcus T. Cicero*

It is great to be great but greater to be human.

It is in giving, not in getting our lives are blessed.

It is in loving not in being loved the heart finds its quest.

It is more blessed to give than to receive.

—*Bible*

It is more necessary to study men than books.

It is never too late to mend.

It is nice to be important but it is more important to be nice.

It is not a secret if it is known by three people.

—*Irish Proverb*

It is not because things are difficult that we dare not venture. It is because we dare not venture that they are difficult.

—*Seneca*

It is not doing the thing we like to do but liking the things we have to do that makes life blessed.

—*Goethe*

It is not enough to aim; you must hit.

—*Italian Proverb*

It is not enough to be superior to some one. What is important is to be superior to one's own former self.

—*Chinmayananda*

It is not every question that deserves an answer.

—*Syrus*

It is not how fast you do a job, but how well you do that matters.

It is not how long but how well we live that matters.

It is not the man who has too little, but the man who craves more that is poor.

—*Seneca*

It is not the place, nor the condition but the mind alone that can make any one happy or miserable.

It is not the size that counts. It is the performance.

It is not what we eat but what we digest that makes us strong.

It is not what we read but what we understand that makes us learned.

It is not what we profess but what we practice.that makes us great.

It is not wide reading but useful reading that leads to excellence.

It is only at tree loaded with fruit that people throw stones.

It is only prudent never to place complete confidence in that by which we have even once been deceived.

—Descartes

It is our responsibilities, not ourselves that we should take seriously.

—Peter Ustinov

It is possible to fail in many ways.... While to succeed is possible only in one way.

—Aristotle

It is possible to make a garden in to a wilderness quickly. But it is not easy to reconstruct the wilderness in to a garden.

It is quality rather than quantity that matters.

—Seneca

It is sure to be dark if you close your eyes.

—Chinmayananda

It is the generous giving of ourselves that produces the generous harvest.

—Marden

It is the heart, the heart that conquers, not the brain.

—Vivekananda

It is the mark of an educated mind to be able to entertain a thought without accepting it.

—Aristotle

It is the wise head that makes the still tongue.

It is through non-hatred alone—by acts of love and understanding that hatred can be overcome.

—Buddha

It is unwise to make foolish commitments.

It is well to give when asked, but it is better to give unasked, through understanding.

—Gibran

It matters not how a man dies, but how he lives.

It takes a lifetime to achieve something; but it takes no time to lose everything completely.

It takes forty muscles to frown and only fifteen to smile.

—Sivananda

J

Judge not according to the appearance.

Justice delayed is justice denied.

K

Keep a definite idea before you and work for it.

Keep a thing for seven years and you will find a use for it.

—Irish Proverb

Keep cool and you command everybody.

Keep five yards from a carriage; then yards from a horse; and a hundred yards from an elephant; but the distance one should keep from a wicked man cannot be measured.

Keep hitting on the same nail top until the nail goes in totally. Never give up.

—G.R. Yugandhar

Keep money but let not money keep you.

Keep your body busy to accomplish things. Keep your mind open to understand things.

—Chinese Proverb

Keep your eyes on a distant star even if it is far away; with faith, courage and hard work you can reach the goal step by step.

Kill not the goose that lays the golden eggs.

—English Proverb

Kind words are benedictions.

Kind words cost nothing.

Kindly smiles and courtesies pay high dividends and their only cost is the persistent endeavor to cultivate them until one has made them a part of one's richest possessions.

—John Savant

Kindness is a language, which the deaf can hear and the blind can read.

Kindness is nobler than revenge.

Know how to listen, and you will profit even from those who talk badly.

Know the true value of time, snatch, seize and enjoy every moment of it.

Knowledge is a treasure but practice is the key to it.

Knowledge is acquired only by the destruction of ignorance.

—*James Allen*

Knowledge is better than wealth. You have to look after wealth. Knowledge looks after you.

Knowledge is not given but earned, and character is not granted but cultivated.

Knowledge is proud that he has learnt so much. Wisdom is humble that he knows no more.

Knowledge makes humble; ignorance makes proud.

L

Lack of involvement and responsibility result in forgetfulness.

Language is the dress of thought.

—*Samuel Johnson*

Laugh and the world laughs with you, weep, you weep alone.

Laugh with others never at them.

Laughing is the sensation of feeling good all over and showing it principally in one spot.

—*Billings*

Laughter is one of the best ways of improving health and relieving stress.

Leadership is the art of getting others want to do something, which you are convinced should be done.

Learn from your mistakes and failures.

Learn how to give without hesitation, how to lose without regret, and how to acquire without meanness.

Learn the art of giving and serving with a smile.

Learning is not attained by chance. It must be sought for with ardor and attended to with diligence.

—*Adams*

Learning to ignore things is one of the great paths to inner peace.

—*Sawyer*

Leave no stone unturned.

—*Euripides*

Leave nothing half finished.

Leave the beaten track occasionally and desire in to the woods, you will be certain to find something you have never seen before.

Let another man praise thee and not thine own mouth.

Let the boat stay on water, but let not the water stay in the boat. So let a man live in the world but let not the world live in him.

Let your inner conscience be your master and your mind your slave.

Liars when speak the truth are not believed.

—*Aristotle*

Life cannot be lived without committing mistakes. What you can do is to admit your mistakes, repent for it, learn from it, rectify the mistake if possible and not to repeat it at any cost.

Life is a bridge, cross over it, but build no house on it.

Life is a game. Play it successfully.

Life is a mixture of success and failures. No rose with out a thorn.

Life is stage and we are all actors.

Life is a strange mixture. We have to take it , as it is, try to understand it, and then to better it.

Life is half spent before we know what it is.

Life is love and sweetest gift from heaven.

Life is neither a tempest nor a mid summer night's dream but it is a comedy of errors and you can do as you like it.

Life is not an empty dream.

Life is not anything; it is only the opportunity to do something.

—*Hebbel*

Life is the holiest and sweetest gift from heaven.

Life is what we make it.

Life means struggle, and the higher you aim, the more you wish to achieve, the greater is the work and sacrifice demanded of you.

—Indira Gandhi

Light comes to individuals through the conscious efforts of their intellect.

—Vivekananda

Listening requires more intelligence than speaking.

Little minds are tamed and subdued by misfortune but great minds rise above it.

Live a clean life.

Live and let live.

Live in the present, neither in the past nor in the future.

Live so that you do not look back and regret that you have wasted you life.

—Kubler Ross

Live such a life that when you die you laugh and others cry.

Live today as best as you can. By living today you will do the most within your power to make tomorrow better.

Live with the wolves, and you learn to howl.

—Spanish Proverb

Look at the contents, not at the bottle.

Look at the ocean and not at the wave.

Look at the positive side in every person and in every thing.

Look before you leap.

Look down if you would know how high you stand.

Look fear in the face and it will cease to trouble you.

Look not mournfully in to the past; it comes not back again; wisely improve the present. —It is thine.

—Longfellow

Look to yourself alone; mind your own business, leaving everyone else to do as he pleases.

Lost time does not return.

—*Kempis*

Love is an act to endless forgiveness, a tender look which becomes a habit.

—*Ustinov*

Love is life and hatred is death.

—*Vivekananda*

Love is that which gives but does not receive. It is doing something good to others with out expecting any reward.

Love is the only antidote to hatred. When you feel like hating a man try to remind yourself that he is a form of your own self.

—*Meher Baba*

Love is the triumph of imagination over intelligence.

—*Menckena*

Love looks not with the eyes, but with the heart.

Love makes all hard hearts gentle.

Love, no doubt is the only solution for man's problem of existence.

—*Chinmayananda*

Love your enemy for they tell your faults.

Love your neighbours, but don't pull down the fence.

—*Chinese Proverb*

Love, pain and money cannot be kept secret; they soon betray themselves.

—*Spanish Proverb*

Loyal words have the secret of healing grief.

—*Menander*

Luck is what happens when preparation meets opportunity.

M

Make a child feel love.

Make hay while the sun shines.

Make the best use of what is in your power and take the rest as it happens.

—Epictetus

Make use of the talent you have.

Make use of time, let not advantage slip.

—Shakespeare

Make your bargain before beginning to plow.

—Arab Proverb

Make yourself lovable and you will be loved by all.

Make yourself master of the business in which you want to succeed.

Make yourself necessary to somebody. Do not make life hard to any.

—Emerson

Making excuses will lead to failure.

Man is but the shadow of God.

Man learns as he lives, and experience is the greatest teacher in the world.

—Vivekananda

Man, the body is mortal but man the soul is immortal.

Man's chiefest treasure is a sparing tongue.

—Hesiod

Man's greatest glory lies not, in never falling but in rising every time he falls.

—Oliver Goldsmith

Manage any conflict in a light and polite manner.

Manage your time as you manage your money.

Management is the art of getting other people to do all the work.

Manifest plainness, embrace simplicity, reduce selfishness, have few desires.

—Leo-tzu

Mankind must put an end to war, or war will put an end to mankind.

—John F. Kennedy

Manners make the man.

Many a friend was lost through a joke, but none was ever gained so.

—Czech Proverb

Many hands make light work.

Many live to eat, the wise eat to live.

Many receive advice; but few profit by it.

—Syrus

Many receive advice; only the wise profit by it.

Many things have fallen only to rise higher.

—Seneca

Measure thrice before you cut once.

Mediocrity can talk; but it is for genius to observe.

Memories are in the heart which none can steal.

Men acquire a particular quality by constantly acting a particular way.... You become just by performing just actions, temperate by performing temperate actions, brave by performing brave actions.

—Aristotle

Men of few words are the best men.

—Shakespeare

Men wear out when idle, just as machines do. Every man is happier when he is working his full hours.

—Henry Ford

Mere accumulation of information or knowledge cannot make a man wise.

Mind employed is mind enjoyed.

Moderation in temper is always a virtue; but moderation in principle is always a vice.

Modesty is the foundation of all virtues. Let your neighbours discover you before you make yourself known to them.

—Zengetsu

Money does not pay nor name; fame does not pay nor learning. It is love that pays; it is character that cleaves its way through adamantine walls of difficulties.

—Vivekananda

Money is a good servant but a bad master.

Moral wealth is the inner wealth, the deeper it is, the less nose it makes.

—Chinmayananda

More grows in the garden than the gardener knows he has sown.

—Spanish Proverb

More haste, less speed.

Most men speak when they do not know how to be silent. He is wise who knows how to hold his peace.

—Ambrose

Motivation is what gets you started. Habit is what keeps you going.

N

Nature has given us two ears, two eyes, and but one tongue, so that, to the end we should hear and see more than we speak.

Nature is the mirror of God.

Necessity does the work of courage.

Necessity is the mother of invention.

—Irish Proverb

Necessity knows no law.

—Irish Proverb

Necessity never made a good bargain.

—North American Proverb

Need teaches a plan.

—Irish Proverb

Negative attitude leads to pessimism.

Neither pleasure nor pain is permanent. They come and go like day and night. It is the happiness born out of awareness that is permanent in the life of man.

Neither under estimate nor over estimate the importance of money, give its due importance.

Never allow others to black mail you.

Never compromise your ideals.

Never cry over spilt milk.

Never cut what can be untied.

—Portuguese Proverb

Never depend upon others too much.

Never do things by halves.

Never do anything when you are in a temper, for you will do everything wrong.

—*Gracian*

Never esteem anything as of advantage to you that will make you break your word or lose your self-respect.

—*Antoninus*

Never forget that the little giving impulses are as important as the big ones more important in a way, for they help you to form the habit of giving yourself away.

—*David Dunn*

Never give advice unless asked.

—*German Proverb*

Never go to excess, but let moderation be your guide.

—*Cicero*

Never grieve for what you cannot help.

Never have too many partners in business.

Never laugh at any one's dreams.

Never promise more than you can perform.

—*Syrus*

Never stand begging for that which you have the power to earn.

—*Cervantes*

Never too late to mend.

Never too late to repent.

Never too old to learn.

Never trouble another for what you can do for yourself.

—*Jefferson*

Never try to appear what you are not.

No act of kindness, no matter how small is ever wasted.

—*Aesop*

No athlete is crowned but in the sweat of his brow.

—*Saint Jerome*

No gains without pains.

No great things were ever done without great labour.

—*Vivekananda*

No legacy is so rich as honesty.

No man is rich whose expenditure exceeds his means and no one is poor whose income exceeds his expenditure.

No man limps because another is hurt.

—*Danish Proverb*

No matter about wearing a crown, make sure that you have a head worthy of wearing one. No matter about a throne on which to sit, make sure that your life is regal in its own intrinsic character.

—*Miller*

No matter what accomplishments you achieve, somebody helps you.

—*Gibson*

No one can become great by mere imitation.

No one can wear a mask for very long.

—*Seneca*

No one is rich enough to do without a neighbour

—*Danish Proverb*

No one knows what he can do till he tries.

—*Syrus*

No pain no gain.

No rose without a thorn.

—*Turkish Proverb*

Nobody is happy all the time. But that is no excuse for being miserable.

None are fair but who are kind.

Not only to say the right thing in the right place, but far

more difficult to leave unsaid the wrong thing at the tempting moment.

Not the cry, but the flight of the wild duck, leads the flock to fly and follow.

—Chinese Proverb

Not the size but the performance that matters.

Nothing can bring you peace except yourself.

—Emerson

Nothing dies faster than a new idea in a closed mind.

Nothing dries sooner than tears.

—Latin Proverb

Nothing great was ever achieved without enthusiasm.

—Emerson

Nothing great was ever done without much endurance.

Nothing happens to anything, which that thing is not made by nature to bear.

—Antoninus

Nothing in this world is difficult to the enterprising.

Nothing is as burdensome as a secret.

—French Proverb

Nothing is ever lost by courtesy. It is the cheapest of the pleasures; costs nothing and conveys much. It pleases him who gives and him who receives and thus like mercy it is twice blessed.

—Wilman

Nothing is impossible to a willing heart.

Nothing is particularly hard if you divide it into small jobs.

—Henry Ford

Nothing is said that has not been said before.

Nothing is so good for an ignorant man as silence; if he were sensible of this he would not be ignorant.

—Saadi

Nothing is so strong as gentleness, nothing so gentle as real strength—the strength of character.

Nothing useless or low. Each thing in its place is best.

—Long Fellow

Nothing ventured, nothing gained.

O

O tongue, be moderate in both eating and talking, for excessive eating and excessive talking both lead to disaster.

Obedience alone gives the right to command.

—Emerson

Obedience is more readily available to the one who commands gently.

Obey the dictates of your conscience.

Obstacles are those frightful things you see when you take your eyes off your goal.

—Henry Ford

Of thy sorrow be not too sad; of thy joy be not too glad.

Of two evils choose the lesser.

Oil and truth get uppermost at last.

On action alone be thy interest, never on its fruits; let not the fruits of action by thy motive, nor be thy attachment to inaction

—Bhagavad Gita

Once the game is over, the king and the pawn go back in the same box.

—Italian Proverb

One bad example spoils many good precepts.

One falsehood leads easily to another.

One flower will not make a garland

—French Proverb

One generation plants the trees another gets the shade.

—*Chinese Proverb*

One hand washes the other.

—*Seneca*

One hour to day is worth two tomorrow.

—*Fuller*

One joy scatters a hundred griefs.

—*Chinese Proverb*

One loss does not make a season.

One must have a good memory to be able to keep the promises one makes.

—*Nietzsche*

One of the advantages of telling the truth is that you don't have to remember what you said.

—*Anonymous*

One of the greatest investments, which we can make is to invest in health for, there is no other investment like it.

—*Mahatma Gandhi*

One of the greatest victories you can gain over someone is to beat him at politeness.

—*Billings*

One pound of learning requires ten pounds of common sense to apply it.

—*Persian Proverb*

One should count each day a separate life.

—*Seneca*

One should examine oneself for a very long time before thinking of condemning others.

One should go invited to a friend is good fortune, and uninvited in misfortune.

—*Swedish Proverb*

One thing well done is twice done.

One who believes that he can conquer will conquer one day.

One who desires the attention of others has not yet found himself.

—Wolbe

One who fears failures limits his activities.

One who knows how to give love is a living God on earth.

Only a fool tests the depth of water with both feet.

Only God is in a position to look down on any one.

—Sarah Brown

Only he can be a leader, who never loses hope.

Only the wearer knows where the shoe pinches.

—English Proverb

Only those who have the patience to do simple things perfectly acquire the skill to do difficult things easily.

—Von Schiller

Opportunity is often lost because of indecision.

Opportunity knocks at the door only once.

Opportunity knocks once, but temptation keeps on banging on the door for all the time.

—Luther

Our deeds are like stones cast into the pool of time, though they themselves may disappear, their ripples extend to eternity.

Our doubts are traitors, and make us lose the good we oft might win by fearing to attempt.

—Shakespeare

Our good and evil deeds follow us continuously like shadows.

Our life is what our thoughts make it.

Our lives become fruitful in giving, but not in getting.

Only shallow men believe in luck.

Our lives teach us who we are.

—Salman Rushdie

Our patience will achieve more than our force.

Our patience will achieve more than our impatience.

Outward rituals and cleanliness without inward purity and devotion is like washing a rotten fruit and eating it.

P

Pain is forgotten where gain follows.

Party is the madness of many, for the gain of a few.

—Joanathan Swift

Patience is a necessary ingredient of a genius.

Patience is bitter but its fruit is sweet.

—French Proverb

Patience is the best remedy for every trouble.

—Plautus

Patience is the greatest of all virtues.

Patience is the key of joy; but haste is the key to sorrow.

—Arabian Proverb

Pay attention to your enemies, for, they are the first to discover your mistakes.

Peace cannot be kept by force. It can only be achieved by understanding.

—Einstein

Peace cannot suddenly descend from the heavens. It can only come when the root causes of trouble are removed.

Peace makes plenty.

People hate the man who loves himself.

People living in glass houses should not throw stones at others.

People who fly in to a rage always make a bad landing.

People who know least talk much and people who know more talk less and listen more.

People with negative attitudes are a liability to others.

People with positive outlook attract others.

Perfect love is that stage where duality disappears. Every thing is seen as part of the whole.

Perfect self-control is a natural trait of an illumined soul

Perfection consists not in doing extraordinary things but in doing ordinary things extraordinarily well.

Perfection is achieved not when there is nothing to add, but when there is nothing left to take away.

Perfection of moral virtue does not wholly take away the passions, but regulates them.

—Saint Thomas Aquinas

Perseverance is the foundation of all success.

Perseverance is the key to success.

Persevere to get perfection.

Personality is the expression of inner life.

Personality is an indefinite thing, a strange force that has power over the souls of men.

Personality is to man what perfume is to flower.

—Schwal

Persuasion is often more effective than force.

—Aesop

Piety requires us to honour truth above our friends.

—Aristotle

Plain dealing is a jewel.

Pleasure in the job puts perfection in the work.

—Aristotle

Pleasure is the flower that fades but remembrance is the perfume that lasts.

Politeness is the flower of humanity. A man who is not polite is not human.

Positive people attract others while negative people repel.

Positive thinking spreads positive energy and it brings happiness not only to the man who possesses it but also the others who are around him.

Pour not water on a drowned mouse.

Pouring oil in to the fire is not the way to quench it.

Poverty does not destroy virtue nor wealth bestows it.

—Anonymous

Power of love is far stronger than love of power.

Practice makes man perfect.

Practise positive thinking until it becomes a habit with you.

Practice what you preach.

Praising all alike is praising none.

Praising yourself is vanity and criticizing yourself is meekness. Avoid both.

Pray to God in a storm, but keep on rowing.

—Danish Proverb

Prayer is when you talk to God; meditation is when you listen to God.

—Diana Robinson

Prevention is better than cure.

Pride goes before a fall.

Pride goeth before destruction and a haughty spirit before a fall.

Pride goeth forth on horse back grand and gay, but cometh back on foot, and begs its way.

—Long Fellow

Pride is at the bottom of all great mistakes.

Pride poisoned with malice becomes envy.

Probability is not proof.

Procrastination is the thief of time.

Procrastination robs you of opportunity.

Project positive thoughts only.

Proper attention and accurate observation lead to good memory.

Provide for the worst, the best will save itself.

Purchase not friends by gifts; when thou ceases to give, such will cease to love.

—*Thomas Fuller*

Put a smile on your face and a firm grip in your handshake.

Put silk on a goat, and it is still a goat.

—*Irish Proverb*

Putting off an easy thing makes it hard, and putting off a hard one makes it impossible.

Q

Quit not certainty for hope.

R

Raise your sail one foot and you get ten feet of wind.

—Chinese Proverb

Reading is to the mind what exercise is to the body.

Reading makes a full man, writing an exact man, speaking a ready man.

—Fracis Bacon

Real love has quality, roots, strength, selflessness, and it always seeks to help; to protect; never to hurt. It does not depend upon rewards. It is simply itself and ennobles any one who is fortunate to have it.

Realisation is the real religion; all the rest is only preparation.

—Vivekananda

Reason is the guide and light of life.

Receiving advice is useless unless you are able to profit by it.

Recognise other's merits.

Reflect on your present blessings, of which every man has many, not on your past misfortunes, of which all men have some.

—Charles Dickens

Refrain from entering in to an argument. Sometimes you may win an argument but in the process lose a friend.

Refrain from giving opinions or suggestions on matters, which you do not know much.

Religion is that secret process which brings forth an

effective personality out of even a shattered man of despair and disappointments.

—Chinmayananda

Remember every act, big or small of kindness done to you.

Remember every promise you have made and keep it up.

Remember the names of people and address them by their names during conversation for bringing about a smooth and cordial relationship with them.

Reputation is what other people know about you, honour is what you know about yourself.

Research is to see what everybody else has seen and to think what no one else has thought.

Resolve the differences with any one smoothly and politely.

Resolve to be tender with the young, compassionate with the aged, sympathetic with the striving and tolerant of the weak and wrong, because, some time in our lives we would have been all of these ourselves.

—Shearer

Respect cannot be commanded but must be earned.

Respect should be earned by actions; and not acquired by years.

Respect yourself and others will respect you.

—Confucius

Responsibilities gravitate to the person who can shoulder them.

—Elbert Hubbard

Return love for hatred.

Reward people with a little more than what they actually deserve.

Riches run after the rich and poverty runs after the poor.

—French Proverb

Rome was not built in a day.

Rudeness is the weak man's imitation of strength.

S

Sacrifice money rather than principles.

Sail in the ship of ambition and anchor in the harbour of success.

Save your time like a miser and you will prove yourself to be wiser.

Say well is good, but do well is better.

Say what is true and what is pleasant. Do not say what is pleasant and not true, nor what is true and not pleasant.

—Anonymous

Scatter with one hand gather with two.

Search others for their virtues, thyself for thy vices.

—Benjamin Franklin

Seeing wise but not seeing much that matters.

Seize opportunity by the beard, for it is bald behind.

—Bulgarian Proverb

Self-conceit may lead to self-destruction.

—Aesop

Self-confidence is the first requisite to great undertakings.

—Samuel Johnson

Self-confidence is the first step to success.

Self-conquest is the greatest of victories.

Self-control is one of the most precious possessions one can have.

Self-help is the first condition of success for a nation, no less than for an individual.

Self-praise is no recommendation.

Self-reliance is an attitude of mind a poor man can be self-reliant while a wealthy person may be dependent on others. Self-reliance means the capacity to make the utmost of what we have and the courage to do without what we do not and we cannot have.

—Lal Bahadur Sastri

Selfless life is a higher way of life than self-centered life.

Selfless service means that it has to be so very natural even the thought that you are serving should be absent.

—Meher Baba

Selflessness, charity, broadmindedness goodness, love, kindness, sympathy, and compassion are the investments you make today for a better, brighter, happy and peaceful tomorrow.

Sell no virtue to purchase wealth, sell no liberty to purchase power.

—Benjamin Franklin

Service is the rent we pay for our room on earth.

Serving God is doing good to man.

—Benjamin Franklin

Set a thief to catch a thief.

Setbacks in life teach us humility.

Shallow men speak of the past, wise men the present, and fools of the future.

Shallow men believe in luck, believe in circumstances, strong men believe in cause and effect.

—Emerson

Sharp words make more wounds than surgeons can heal.

Silence and reserve suggest latent power; what some men think has more effect than what others say.

—Chesterfield

Silence is an excellent remedy against slander.

Silence is less injurious than a bad reply.

Silence is not always golden; some times it is guilt.

Silence is one of the hardest arguments to refute.

—Billings

Silence is the best reply to the ignorant.

—Persian Proverb

Silence is the ornament and safeguard of the ignorant.

Silence seldom doth harm.

Silence when nothing need be said, is the eloquence of discretion.

—Bovee

Simplicity and reserve lead to beauty and truth.

Since we cannot get what we like, let us like what we can get.

—Spanish Proverb

Slight not what's near, while aiming at what's far.

—Euripides

Slow and steady wins the race.

—Aesop

Small communities grow great through harmony; great ones fall to pieces through discord.

—Sallust

Small deeds done are better than great deeds planned.

Small opportunities are often the beginning of great enterprises.

—Demosthenes

Small showers last long, but sudden storms are short.

Soft words win hard hearts.

—Benham

Some one will always be looking at you as an example of how to behave. Don't let him down.

Some people are masters of money, and some its slaves.

Something is better than nothing.

Spare the rod and spoil the child.

—*Old Proverb*

Spare when you are young and spend when you are old.

Speak kind words and you will hear kind echoes.

Speak not every truth, for that is unneedful.

Speech is human; silence is divine.

Speech is silver. Silence is golden.

Spend less time worrying who is right and more time deciding what is right.

Spend within your means to keep away from troubles and disaster.

Start your day with a smile on your face and gratitude for the blessings in your heart.

Stop worrying about the potholes in the road. Celebrate the journey.

Straight-forwardness without civility is like a surgeon's knife, effective but unpleasant.

—*Si Yukteshwar*

Strength is life weakness is death.

—*Vivekananda*

Stress is an ignorant state; it believes that everything is an emergency.

Strike while the iron is hot.

Strive for excellence however small the task is.

Success comes not in the absence of problems but inspite of problems.

Success does not mean the absence of failures, it means the attainment of ultimate objectives, it means winning the war, not every battle.

—*Edwin C. Bliss*

Success does not have elevators; it has only steps.

Success in marriage is much more than finding the right person; it is a matter of being the right person.

Success is a journey, not a destination.

Success is a marathon, not a sprint.

Success is having the courage to meet failure without being defeated.

Success is the culmination of hard work and thorough preparation.

—*Lobsang Rampa*

Success is the progressive realisation of a worthy goal.

—*Earl Nightingale*

Success is the result of punctuality, enough preparation, accuracy, hard work, ambition, enthusiasm, and commonsense.

Success is the result of right decisions at the right time.

Success is the sum of small efforts repeated day in and day out.

Success is worthwhile only when it is achieved by fair and honest means.

Success often comes to those who dare and act. It seldom goes to the timid who are ever afraid of the consequences.

Success requires lot of sacrifice and self-discipline.

Suffering puts the ego in its place and forces it to turn to the divine for help.

Suicide is a permanent solution to a temporary problem.

Superior man is satisfied and composed; the mean man is always full of distress.

—*Confucius*

Surrounding yourself with dwarfs does not make you a giant.

—*Yiddish Saying*

Suspicion is the poison of friendship.

Sweet are the uses of adversity.

Tact is the knack of making a point without making an enemy.

—Isaac Newton

Take care of minutes, for the hours will take care of themselves.

—Chesterfield

Take the rough with the smooth.

Take time for laugh. It helps to lift life's worries.

Take time when time cometh, lest time steal away.

Talent hits a target no one else can hit; Genius hits a target no one else can see.

—Shopenhaurer

Talking comes by nature, silence by wisdom.

Talking is sharing, but listening is caring.

Target the stars, in case you miss the target, you will reach the clouds.

Teachers open the door. You enter by yourself.

—Chinese Proverb

Tell me who you live with and I will tell you who you are.

—Spanish Proverb

Tell the truth and shame the devil.

That best portion of a good man's life-his little, nameless, unremembered acts of kindness and of love.

—William Shakespeare

That man is disciplined and happy who can prevail over the turmoil that springs from desire and anger, here on earth, before he leaves his body.

That man is a hero who can make friend of a foe.

That man is the richest whose pleasures are the cheapest.

—Thoreau

That which is worth doing is worth finishing. Do not give up in the middle.

The abundance of money ruins youth.

The actions of men are like the index of a book; they point out what is more remarkable in them.

—Thomas

The activist is not the man who says the river is dirty. The activist is the man who clears up the river.

The acts of this life are the destiny of the next.

The arrow belongs not to the archer when it has once left the bow; the word no longer belongs to the speaker when it has once passed his lips.

The basic difference between an ordinary man and a warrior is that a warrior takes everything as a challenge, while an ordinary man takes everything either as a blessing or a curse.

—Don Juan

The beauty of a home is harmony; the security of a house is loyalty; the joy of a house is love; the plenty of a house is children; the rule of the house is service; the comfort of a house is in contented spirits; the maker of a house of a real human house is God, Himself, the same who made the stars and built the world.

—Frank Crane

The beginning of all great things were small.

The best and safest thing is to keep a balance in your life, acknowledge the great powers around us and in us. If you can do that, and live that way, you are really a wise man.

—Euripides

The best doctors are Dr. Diet, Dr. Quiet and Dr. Merry man.

—Jonathan Swift

The best of all medicines are rest and fasting.

—Benjamin Franklin

The best portion of a good man's life is his little, nameless, unremembered acts of kindness and of love.

—William Wordsworth

The best teachers of humanity are the lives of great men.

—Q.S. Flower

The best tranquilizer is a clear conscience.

The best victory is the victory over the mind.

The best way to cheer your self up is to try to cheer somebody else up.

The best way to convince a fool that he is wrong is to let him have his own way.

—Josh Billings

The best way to punish a person who has done a harm to us is to do some good to him so that the feels ashamed for what he had done to us.

—Tirukkural

The body is a sacred garment.

—Martha Graham

The body says what words cannot.

—Martha Graham

The books, which help you most are those which make you think the most.

—Theodo Parker

The capacity to endure is sometimes the best way to meet fear and worry.

—Preston Bradley

The cause is hidden. The effect is visible to all.

—Ovid

The charity that hastens to proclaim its good deeds ceases

to be charity, and is only pride and ostentation

—William Hutton

The chief ingredients in the composition of those qualities that gain esteem and praise are good nature, truth, good sense, and good breeding.

—Addison

The clock of life is wound but once.

—Anonymous

The crown and glory of life is character.

The crown of a good disposition is humility.

—Arab Proverb

The darkest hour is that before the dawn.

—Proverb

The defects of great men are the consolation of the dunces.

The dictionary is the only place where success comes before work.

The divine with holds everything till the time is ripe.

—Mahabharatha

The early bird catches the worm.

The easiest way to dignity is humility.

The echo of Love is nothing but Love.

The evening of a well-spent life brings its lamps with it.

The eye that sees all things else sees not itself.

The face is the mirror of the mind, and eyes without speaking confers the secrets of the heart.

—Saint Jerome

The fact speaks for themselves.

—Domesthenes

The fear of war is worse than war itself.

The finger of accusation is no part of the helping hand.

The firm, the enduring, the simple and the modest are near to virtue.

—Confucius

The first step to a good name is a good life; and the next is good behaviour.

The first step towards amendment is the recognition of error.

—Seneca

The first step to knowledge is to know that you are ignorant.

The first step in the discipline of the mind is the overcoming of indolence.

—James Allen

The first wealth is health

—Emerson

The fool does think he is wise, but the wise man knows himself to be a fool.

—William Shakespeare

The fool is busy in everybody's business but his own.

The fool wanders, the wise man travels.

The foundation of a lasting victory can only be laid on the rock of truths.

The gem cannot be polished without friction, nor man perfected without trials.

—Chinese Proverb

The girl who cannot dance says the band cannot play.

—Yeddish Proverb

The glory of man can never last long, but the glory of God is eternal.

The good is secured only by abandoning the evil.

—James Allen

The greatest hunger a person has is to be needed. Help create that feeling in others.

The greatest mischief-maker is the human tongue.

The greatest remedy for anger is delay.

—Seneca

The greatest test of courage on earth is to bear defeat with out losing heart.

—Ingersol

The greatest truths are the simplest; and so are the greatest men.

—Hare

The greatest virtue is kindness. You can't love every one but you can be kind to every one.

The greatest wealth is contentment with a little.

The greatness of a man is never better disclosed than in self-restraint.

—S. Radhakrishnan

The habit of common and continuous speech is a symptom of mental deficiency.

—Walter Bagehot

The hand that rocks the cradle rules the world.

The happiness of a man in this life does not consist in the absence but in the mastery of his passions.

—Tennyson

The harder the conflict, the more glorious the triumph.

The heart has its reason's which reason knows not of.

—Pascal

The heart of the fool is in his mouth, but the mouth of the wise man is in his heart.

—Franklin

The heights that great men reached and kept were not attained by sudden flight; but they, while their companions slept, were toiling upward in the night.

—Long Fellow

The highest form of grace is silence.

—Chinmayananda

The history of the world is full of men who rose to leadership by sheer force of self-confidence, bravery, and tenacity.

—Gandhi

The human life is a great gift from God. It should be valued as such and used for sacred purpose.

The key to every thing is patience. You get the chicken by hatching the egg, not by smashing it.

The kingdom of God is within you.

The light heart lives long.

—Irish Proverb

The man who goes furthest is generally the one who is willing to do and dare.

—Dale Carnegie

The man who does not know how to think does not know how to live.

The man who has received a benefit ought always to remember it, but he who has granted it ought to forget the fact at once.

—Demosthenes

The man who removes a mountain begins by carrying away small stones.

The man with the boots does not mind where he places his foot.

—Irish Proverb

The manner of giving is worth more than the gift.

The measure of life is its excellence, not its length.

—Plato

The mind uncontrolled and unguided will drag us down for ever.

—Vivekananda

The more a man knows the more he forgives.

—Anonymous

The more arguments you win, the fewer friends you will have.

The more faithfully you listen to the voice within you, the better you will hear what is sounding outside and only he who listens can speak.

—Dag Hammerskjold

The more you give the more you are bound to receive. The more you know, the more you have to learn.

—Lobsang Rampa

The more you speak of yourself the more you are likely to lie.

The most meaningful kindness is often reflected in the smallest things of every day life.

—Jesse Chiang

The most peaceful place in which to live is within one's income.

—Bernard Shaw

The most wasted of all days is that one which has not laughed.

The nail that sticks up will be hammered down.

—Japanese Proverb

The noblest vengeance is to forgive.

The old order changed yielding place to new.

The one who is mad after the Divine forgets the worldly things and the one who is mad after the worldly things forgets the Divine.

The one who uses the word 'I' the least is liked by all.

The only conquests, which are permanent and leave no regrets, are our conquests over ourselves.

—Napolean

The only good luck many great men ever had was being born with the ability and determination to overcome bad luck.

The only man who never makes a mistake is the man who never does anything.

—Theodor Roosewelt

The only stable state is the one in which all men are equal before the law.

—Aristotle

The only truly happy people are those who have found some one, some cause to love and belong to.

—John Powell

The palest ink is better than the best memory.

—Chinese Proverb

The parent's life is the child's copy—book.

The pine stays green in winter. Wisdom in hardship.

The price of greatness is responsibility.

—Winston Churchill

The price of success is hard work.

—Visvesvarayya

The pride of youth is in strength and beauty, the pride of old age is in discretion.

—Democritus

The proof of the pudding is in its eating.

The real character of a man is revealed in adversity.

The real dignity of a man lies not in what he has; but in what he is.

The real knowledge is the knowledge that God is the inner dweller is good people and the so-called bad, in saint and the so-called sinner. Harm no one is thought word or deed.

The reason we have two ears and only one mouth is that we may hear more and speak less.

—Zeno

The result of every work is mixed with good and evil. You should encourage such works, which bring the largest amount of good and the smallest measure of evil.

—Vivekananda

The reverse side also has a reverse side.

—Japanese Proverb

The riches that are in the heart cannot be stolen.

—Russian Proverb

The right man comes at the right time.

—Italian Proverb

The road to a friend's house is never long.

—Danish Proverb

The root cause of anger is ignorance and egoism.

—Sivananda

The scars of others should teach us caution.

—Saint Jerome

The secret of being a bore is to tell everything.

—Voltaire

The secret of happiness lies in the realisation that we do not live for ourselves alone. We live for the good of others as much as of our own selves.

The secret of life is not to do what you like but to like what you do.

The self-mastery gives man freedom from his slavery to circumstances and no more does he ever come under the lashes of failure or sorrow.

—Chinmayananda

The shifts of fortune test the reliability of friends.

—Cicero

The shortest way to do many things is to do only one thing at a time.

—Cecil

The shortest, easiest, and the best way out of difficulty is through it.

The silent dog is the first to bite.

—German Proverb

The sky is of the same colour wherever you go.

—Persian Proverb

The small courtesies sweeten life; the greater ennoble it.

The smallest deed is greater than the grandest intention.

The smile that lights the face will also warm the heart-Keep smiling.

The superior man..does not set his mind either for anything, or against anything; what is right he will follow.

—*Confucius*

The supreme art of living is to strive to live each day well.

The test of courage comes when we are in the minority; the test of tolerance comes when we are in the majority.

The test of courage is the bearing of defeat without losing heart.

—*R.G. Ingersol*

The tiniest dew drop hanging from a grass blade in the morning is big enough to reflect the sun shine and blue of the sky.

The tongue is more to be feared than the sword.

—*Japanese Proverb*

The tongue is to be used moderately both for eating and talking to avoid disaster.

The tongue like a sharp knife kills without drawing blood.

—*Chinese Proverb*

The tragedy of human history is decreasing happiness in the midst of increasing comforts.

—*Chinmayananda*

The tree casts its shade upon all, even the woodcutter.

The true civilization is where everyman gives to every other every right that he claims for himself.

—*Ingersoll*

The true measure of a man is how he treats someone who can do him absolutely no good.

—*Samuel Johnson*

The true road to success in any field is to make yourself the master in that field.

The truly great is he who knows when to yield and when to stand firm.

The unspoken word never does harm.

The value of experience is not in seeing much, but in seeing wisely.

The willingness to disappear from gaze, the utter absence of self-seeking is the hallmark of greatness.

The wise adapt themselves to circumstances, as water moulds itself to the pitcher.

—*Chinese Proverb*

The wise man, before he speaks, will consider well, what he speaks, to whom he speaks and where and when.

—*St. Ambrose*

The wise man has long ears, big eyes, and a short tongue.

—*Russian Proverb*

The wise man sits on the hole in his carpet.

—*Persian Proverb*

The yes man is your enemy; but you friend will argue with you.

The Zenith of pride is arrogance and it is the root cause for the downfall of man.

There are many paths to the top of the mountain, but the view is always the same.

—*Chinese Proverb*

There are no menial jobs; only menial attitudes.

—*William Bennett*

There are those who give and know not pain in giving, nor do they seek joy nor give with mindfulness of virtue. Through the hands of such as these God speaks and from behind their eyes. He smiles upon the earth.

—*Prophet*

There is a time for all things.

—*William Shakespeare*

There is not better looking—glass than an old friend.

There is no dignity quite so impressive and no independence quite so important as living within you means.

There is no elevator to success. You have to take the stairs.

There is no one luckier than he who thinks himself so.

—German Proverb

There is no permanent success in tricky methods.

There is no possession more precious than self-control.

There is no repayment for such a thing as affection.

There is no revenge so complete as forgiveness.

—Josh Billings

There is no strength without unity.

There is no venom as sharp as the venom of the tongue.

There is nothing better than contagious laughter.

There is nothing new under the sun but there are lots of old things we do not know.

There is nothing that wastes the body like worry.

—Gandhi

There is plenty of sound in an empty barrel.

—Russian Proverb

There's many a slip between the cup and the lip.

—Greek Proverb

They alone live who live for others.

—Vivekananda

They are the weakest, however strong who have no faith in themselves or their powers.

They can conquer who believe they can.

—Virgil

They serve God well, who serve his creatures.

Things that are done, it is needless to speak about....things that are past, it is needless to blame.

—Confucius

Think big and act big.

Think big and your deeds will grow; think small and you will fall behind.

—Wilsay

Think like a man of action and act like a man of thought.

—Henry Bergson

Think of long-term results but not short-term benefits.

Think of your work only when it is being done, both before and not after.

—The Mother

Think positively.

Thinking is the essence of wisdom.

—Persian Proverb

Thinking well is wise, planning well is wiser, and doing well is wisest.

Those intent on prospering in life must surely do away with laziness.

—Thiruvalluvar

Though familiarity may not breed contempt it takes off the edge of admiration.

Though we are slaves of the past, we are masters of the future.

Though you are bound to love your enemy you are not bound to put your sword in his hand.

Thought is all-important, for, what we think we become.

—Vivekananda

Three things to give; alms to the needy, comfort to the afflicted, and appreciation to the worthy.

Time and money should be managed wisely.

Time and tide wait for no man.

Time cannot be expanded, accumulated mortgaged, hastened, or retarded.

—Benjamin Franklin

Time is one of heaven's richest gifts and once lost is irrecoverable.

—Lord Avebury

Time is the wisest counselor.

—Pericles

Time is the school in which we learn.

Time like life can never be recalled.

—Benjamin Franklin

Time lost is never gained.

Time will make you shine, in case you do not waste time.

To acquire wealth is difficult, to preserve it more difficult, but to spend it wisely most difficult of all.

To be angry is to revenge the faults of others on ourselves.

—Chinmayananda

To be good and successful at the same time, maintain a perfect balance between the dictates of the head and the heart.

To be feared is to fear; no one has been able to strike terror in to others and at the same time enjoy peace of mind.

—Seneca

To be good and to do good, that is the whole of religion.

—Vivekananda

To be happy we need to concentrate on happy thoughts.

To be lonely without being alone is bitter loneliness. To be alone without being lonely is sweet solitude.

—Jesse Chiang

To be loved, be lovable.

—Ovid

To be loyal to a comrade, or to a cause is certainly a virtue.

To be perfectly just is an attribute of the divine nature, to be so to the utmost of our abilities is the glory of man.

—Joseph Addison

To be spiritual is not to reject reason but to go beyond it.

—S. Radhakrishnan

To be successful in business, be doing, be first, be different.

—William Mercant

To be successful in business, have a definite idea before you, think of it constantly, have a clear-cut plan and work for it.

To climb steep hills requires slow pace at first.

—William Shakespeare

To cultivate kindness is a valuable art of the business of life.

To do easily what is difficult for others is the mark of talent. To do what is impossible for talent is the mark of genius.

—Arriel

To do injustice is more disgraceful than to suffer it.

To do two things at once is to do neither.

—Syrus

To err is human; to forgive is divine.

—Alexander Pope

To gain something we have to lose something. But always make sure that what you lose is worth the gaining.

To give and not to count the cost, to fight and not to heal the wounds, to toil and not to seek rest, to labour and not to ask for reward—This is the way to lead an ideal life.

To give love is nobler than to receive love.

—Chinmayananda

To give love is true freedom. To demand love is pure slavery.

—Chinmayananda

To handle yourself use your head, to handle others use your heart.

To harken to evil conversation is the road to wickedness.

—Anonymous

To have a definite aim in life is to create a source of energy that will sweep away all obstacles.

To have a friend, you must be a friend starting with yourself.

To improve your actions purify your thoughts and to purify your thoughts perform noble deeds.

To know that you do not know is the best. To pretend to know when you do not know is a disease.

—Lao-tzu

To know the road ahead, ask those coming back.

—Chinese Proverb

To know what you know, and to know what you do not know, is the characteristic of one who knows.

—Confucius

To lend is to buy a quarrel.

—Proverb

To live in hearts what we leave behind is not to die.

—Anonymous

To love and to be loved is the greatest happiness of existence.

—Chinmayananda

To read without reflecting is like eating without digesting.

—Edmund Burk

To remain young we must be active. A still pond of water stagnates but not the river.

To see may be easy; but to foresee, that is the great thing

To see tings in the seed, that is genius.

—Laotzu

To talk without thinking is to shoot without aiming.

—Proverb

To teach is to learn.

—Japanese Proverb

To wish to be well is a part of becoming well.

—Seneca

Too many cooks spoil the broth.

Too much rest is rust.

—Sir Walter Scott

To often we underestimate the power of a touch, a smile, a kind word, a listening ear, an honest compliment, or the smallest act of caring all of which have the potential to turn a life around.

—Leo Buscaglia

Too soft and you will be squeezed; too hard you will be broken.

—Arabic Proverb

Train up a fig tree in the way it should go, and when you are old sit under the shade of it.

—Charles Dickens

True happiness consists in making others happy.

—Plato

True happiness consists not in the multitude of friends but in their worth and value.

—Ben Johnson

True heroism is remarkably sober, very undemocratic. It is not the urge to surpass all others at whatever cost, but the urge to serve others at whatever cost.

—Arthur Ashe

True knowledge is modest and wary. It is ignorance that is bold and presuming.

True merit, like a mirror, the deeper it is, the less noise it makes.

True nobility is effortless and natural.

True self-interest teaches selflessness.

True silence is rest of the mind; it is to the spirit what sleep is to the body; nourishment and refreshment.

—William Penn

True wisdom consists not only in seeing what is before your eyes but in foreseeing what is to come.

Trust in God and do what is right.

Trust not a new friend nor an old enemy.

Trust your self. You know more than you think you do.

Truth and oil always come to the surface.

—*Spanish Proverb*

Truth is the secret of eloquence and of virtue, the basis of moral authority; it is the highest summit of art and life.

Truth is to the ears what smoke is to the eyes and vinegar to the teeth.

—*German Proverb*

Trying harder does not always work. Try smarter.

Try to be self-reliant. To much dependence on others will weaken the body, mind, and intellect.

Try to view everything objectively; you will not find fault with any thing or anybody.

Two things indicate weakness—to be silent when it is proper to speak and to speak when it is proper to be silent.

—*Persian Proverb*

U

Unborn tomorrow, dead yesterday, why fret if today be sweet.

—Omar Khayam

Undertake any task after proper consultation, consideration and decision and then execute it with strong resolution.

Uneasy lies the head that wears a crown.

—William Shakespeare

Union is strength.

Unless you enter the tiger's den you cannot take the cubs.

—Japanese Proverb

Unselfishness is more paying; only people have not the patience to practice it.

—Vivekananda

Until you try you do not know what you cannot do.

—Henry James

Unto the pure all things are pure.

—Old Testament

Use soft words and hard arguments.

Use your hands for worldly goods and your head for heavenly thoughts.

Use your talents not only for yourself but also for helping the less fortunate.

Utilise the present to its fullest for an assured better future.

V

Violence is the last refuge of the incompetent.

Virtue and genuine graces in themselves speak what no words can utter.

—William Shakespeare

Virtues are the fruits of self discipline and do not drop from heaven of themselves as does rain or snow.

—Zengetzu

W

Want a thing long enough and you don't.

—Chinese Proverb

Waste not fresh tears over old griefs.

—Euripides

Waste not want not.

Way to wealth is industry and frugality.

We advance ourselves as we help others. The more we help others, the more we receive in return.

—Percy Greaves Jr.

We are as happy as we make up our minds to be.

We are responsible for what we are and whatever we wish ourselves to be, we have the power to make ourselves.

—Vivekananda

We are what we have made and our future is made by us now.

—Mahaveera

We are what we repeatedly do.

—Aristotle

We cannot help ourselves without helping others.

—Jannett Cole

We cannot prosper without bringing prosperity to others.

—Jannet Cole

We can't take any credit for our talents. It's how we use them that counts.

We come nearest to the great when we are great in humility

—Tagore

We cough to clear our throats. We sigh to clear our hearts.

—T.S. Mathews

We give of ourselves when we give gifts of the heart, love, kindness, joy, understanding, sympathy, tolerance, and forgiveness.

—David Dunn

We judge ourselves by what we feel capable of doing; while others judge us by what we have already done.

—Long Fellow

We judge ourselves by our capabilities. Others judge us by our achievements.

We learn and grow and are transformed not so much by what we do but by what and how we do it.

We must always listen to criticisms of our faults and failings, never to our praises.

—Gandhiji

We must be patient with others and impatient only with ourselves.

—S. Radhakrishnan

We must embrace pain and burn it as fuel for our journey.

We must first govern ourselves before we can govern others.

—S. Radhakrishnan

We only get what we deserve.

—Vivekananda

We reap what we sow.

We squander health in search of wealth. We scheme and toil and save; then squander wealth in search of health and all we get is a grave.

—Anonymous

We tell our triumphs to the crowds, but our own hearts are the sole confidants of our sorrow.

We'll never know the worth of water till the well go dry.

—Scottish Proverb

Wealth is the slave of a wise man. The master of a fool.

—Seneca

Well begun is half done.

We done is better than well said.

—Benjamin Franklin

Well-timed silence has more eloquence than speech.

Well-timed silence is the most commanding expression.

What a man thinks of himself determines his fate.

What belongs to everybody belongs to nobody.

—Spanish Proverb

What breaks in a moment may take years to mend.

—Swedish Proverb

What cannot be cured must be endured.

What is important is not to make the best decision but to make a better one each time.

—Johnson

What lies behind us and what lies before us are tiny matters compared to what lies within us.

—Emerson

What makes life worth living is our giving and forgiving.

—Springer

What may be done at any time will be done at no time.

What one does, one becomes.

—Spanish Proverb

What readily yielded to courtesy is never yielded to force.

—Gandhi

What sunshine is to flowers, smiles are to humanity.

—Addison

What tne superior man seeks is in himself; What the small man seeks is in others.

—Confucius

What the world really needs is more love and less paper work.

What we get cheaply we value lightly; it is dearness that gives everything its value.

What we must know is how we are valuable rather than how valuable we are.

What you cannot avoid, welcome.

—Chinese Proverb

What you do not want others to do to you, do not do for others.

—Confucius

What you eat and what you think is what you are.

—Linda Goodman

What you keep to yourself, you lose, what you give away you keep forever.

Whatever you can do, or dream you can, begin it. Boldness has genius, power and magic in it.

—Goethe

Whatever you undertake, act with prudence, and consider the consequences.

—Anonymous

When a man gives way to anger, he only harms himself.

When a twig grows hard it is difficult to twist it.

—Irish Proverb

When anger rises, think of the consequences.

—Confucius

When fortune knocks at the door, open it widely.

—Spanish Proverb

When one dog barks another will join it.

—Latin Proverb

When principles are at stake be stronger than thunder.

When sorrow is asleep wake it not.

When spider webs unite, they can tie up a lion.

—Ethiopian Proverb

When the character of man is not clear to you, look at his friends.

—Japanese Proverb

When the fruit grows out of the flower the petals drop off themselves. Similarly when the divinity in you increases, the weakness of your human nature will all vanish of their own accord.

—Ramakrishna Paramahamsa

When the one great scorer comes to write against your name, he marks not that you won or lost—but how you played the game.

—Grantland Rice

When the stomach is full, it is easy to talk of fasting.

—Saint Jerome

When there is no enemy within the enemies outside cannot hurt you.

—African Proverb

When there is order in the nation, there will be peace in the world.

—Chinese Proverb

When there is peace with in, there is peace without.

When we sing everybody hears us, when we sigh nobody hears us.

—Russian Proverb

When words fail, music speaks.

When you drink the water, remember the spring.

—Chinese Proverb

When you have given nothing, ask of nothing.

—Albanian Proverb

When you shoot an arrow of truth dip its prints in honey.

When you show kindness be softer than the flower.

When you speak make it a point to listen to yourself.

When you think of giving advice, place your teeth before you tongue.

—*Bulgarian Proverb*

When you were born, you cried and the world rejoiced. Live your life so that when you die, the world cries and you rejoice.

When your enemy falls, don't rejoice—but don't pick him up either.

—*Yiddish Proverb*

Where boasting ends, there dignity begins.

Where charity and wisdom are there is neither fear nor ignorance.

Where the river is the deepest it makes the least sound.

—*Italian Proverb*

Where there is a will there is a way.

Whether you think you can or think you can't, you are right.

—*Henry Ford*

While the cat's away, the mice can play.

Whilst we deliberate how to begin a thing, it grows too late to begin it.

—*Quintilian*

Who begins too much accomplishes little.

—*German Proverb*

Who ever gossips to you will gossip about you.

—*Spanish Proverb*

Who knows most speaks least.

—*Spanish Proverb*

Who lies with dogs shall rise up with fleas.

—*Latin Proverb*

Who raises from prayer a better man, his prayer is answered.

—*George Meredith*

Why kill time when one can empty it?

—*French Proverb*

Why worry and get wrinkles, better smile and get dimples.

Wisdom lies in knowing when to speak and when to be silent.

—*Buddha*

Wisdom not knowledge that makes a man happy.

Wise men learn by other men's mistakes, fools by their own.

—*H.G. Bohn*

Wise men talk because they have something to say; fools, because they have to say something

—*Plato*

With foxes we must play the fox.

—*Thomas Fuller*

With money you are a dragon; with no money, a worm.

—*Chinese Proverb*

With our thoughts we make the world.

—*Buddha*

With regard to excellence, it is not enough to know, but we must try to have and use it.

—*Aristotle*

Wonder is the beginning of wisdom.

—*Greek Proverb*

Words coming from the mouth are ordinary, words coming from the throat are genuine and words coming from the heart are divine.

Work and rest must alternate.

Work out step by step towards each goal.

Work while you have the light.

Worry often gives a small thing a big shadow.

—*Swedish Proverb*

Write a wise saying and your name will live for ever.

—*Anonymous*

Write down the advice of him who loves you, though you like it or not at present.

Write injuries in sand, kindness in marble.

—*French Proverb*

Write it on your heart that everyday is the best day in the year.

—*Emerson*

Y

Yesterday is a cancelled cheque. Tomorrow is a promissory note. Today is ready cash. Use it.

Yesterday is but a dream. Tomorrow is only a vision. But today well-lived make every yesterday a dream of happiness, and every tomorrow a vision of hope.

You are as young as your faith, as old as your doubt and as young as your self-confidence and hope, as old as your fear and despair.

You are judged by what you do now but not what you did yesterday or what you will do tomorrow.

You can make more friends in two months by becoming interested in other people than you can in two years by trying to get other people interested in you.

—Dale Carnegie

You can only be young once. But you can always be immature.

You can preach a better sermon with your life than with your lips.

—Oliver Goldsmith

You can take no credit for beauty at sixteen. But if you are beautiful at sixty, it will be your soul's own doing.

—Marie Stopes

You can't cross the sea merely by standing and staring at the water.

You can't hatch chickens from fried eggs.

—Dutch Proverb

You can't have the cake and eat it too

You can't shake hands with a clinched fist.

—Indira Gandhi

You can't stop the birds of sadness to pass over your head, but you can prevent them from resting in your hair.

You cannot escape the responsibility of tomorrow by evading it today.

—Abraham Lincoln

You cannot bring prosperity by discouraging thrift; you cannot strengthen the weak by weakening the strong; you cannot enrich the poor by impoverishing the rich; you cannot establish sound security on borrowed money; you cannot help the wage earner by putting down the wage payer; you cannot build character and courage by taking away man's initiative and independence, you cannot further the brotherhood of man by inciting class hatred; you cannot keep out of trouble by spending more than you earn; you cannot help men permanently by doing for them what they could and should do for themselves.

—Abraham Lincoln

You don't have to be great to start, but you have to start to be great.

You get what you pay for.

You get what you speak; you are what you think; you 'am' what you conclude.

—Ramtha

You have greater impact on others by the way you listen than by the way you talk.

You have to allow a certain amount of time in which you are doing nothing in order to have things occur to you, to let your mind think.

—Adler

You keep money, but let not money keep you.

You may be disappointed if you fail but you are doomed if you don't try.

You may have to fight a battle more than once to win it.

You must have long-range goals to keep you from being frustrated by short-range failures.

—*Charles C. Noble*

You must lose a fly to catch a trout.

—*George Herbert*

You never know your luck unless you try.

You serve yourself when you serve another.

You will never find time for anything. If you want time you must make it.

—*Charles Buxton*

You've got to do your own growing, no matter how tall your grand father was.

—*Irish Proverb*